VANISHING POINTS

STEAM IN WORCESTERSHIRE

ERIC E. PRICE
33 35, VISCOUNT COBHAM COURT,
PICKERSLEIGH ROAD,
MALVERN,
WORCS. WR14 2RJ
TEL: 01684 576570

VANISHING POINTS

STEAM IN WORCESTERSHIRE   *MICHAEL DOWTY*

ALAN SUTTON
1986

ALAN SUTTON PUBLISHING
BRUNSWICK ROAD · GLOUCESTER

First published 1986

British Library Cataloguing in Publication Data

Vanishing points: steam in Worcestershire.
1. Railroads — England —
Worcestershire — History — 20th
century
I. Dowty, Michael
385'.09424'4   HE 3019.W/

ISBN 0-86299-286-9

Printed in Great Britain

Introduction

As one who has met many railmen, experts, enthusiasts, modellers and spotters over a number of years, I have remained remarkably unimproved in matters of railway knowledge. Surprisingly, my comparative ignorance has remained undetected – unless those concerned have been too polite to tell me that it showed. My interest has primarily been the visual one, from the standpoint of the good layman who doesn't know much about the subject but likes what he sees. When the GW150 Exhibition Train visited Worcester this year, I was erroneously introduced to someone as 'a local authority on railways' and was duly relieved at having left my blushing days far behind me.

You will have quickly gathered that you are not in for a feast of railway erudition. What follows is a miscellany of pictorial gleanings, spanning thirty-odd years. There are gaps in the periods of time and locations covered, as there are variations in the degree of coverage, largely through the intervention of other commitments. Even at the height of my railway activities it was not always possible to be at the right place at the right time. There were many frustrations, but compensations too, as on the closure day at Bromyard, when, having crawled all the way behind a Midland Red bus in early morning fog, I found that the train had been held back in anticipation of my arrival, so that I might obtain some sort of hazy record of its final disappearance (see top of page 38). This was typical of the attitude of all those with whom I came into contact; regardless of their bleak prospects, they were, without exception, courteous, eager to help and not once did they lose a shred of their dignity. It made one feel ashamed and saddened that such good men were about to be scrapped, together with their locomotives and stations, in the cause of some dubious exercise in economics.

Progress is too often in the hands of those with 'megalomanic' tendencies. Not content with modifying one part of the system at a time, they have a built-in compulsion to instantly devastate all they can get their hands on. Twenty or more years after the axe, we look in vain for any real halt in the decline of rail services. It is now possible to get from A to B very quickly, but since it is impossible to reach A in the first place, it doesn't really help all that much, unless, in the more than likely absence of a reliable bus service, the passenger has a car, and if he has a car he either won't need or won't be able to afford train travel. I recently read a wonderfully shrewd observation by George Mikes, the Hungarian-born humorist, who wrote, recalling his arrival in this country many years ago: 'Then, only the rich man could afford a car; now, only the rich man can afford to be without one.'

The bulk of my photographs concern the Beeching and post-Beeching eras. Personally, I always felt that the then Dr Beeching came in for some not wholly justified criticism. He was, after all, only ruthlessly administering a strategy that had been fabricated elsewhere. My own feelings of animosity were more for Ernest Marples, for one particularly fatuous utterence in respect of a proposed closure. He stated that he felt it would be better to buy all the passengers motor-scooters, rather than maintain the line. Carried to its conclusion, this supreme logic would have seen the end of the police force and the fire service and have had us all scootering around with truncheons, whistles and fire-extinguishers.

It is easy to see why there is an abundance of railway nostalgia. Those of us who grew up with a steam train service, used it, watched it, heard it and smelt it, know that part of our way of life has gone for ever. It may not necessarily have been the quickest, cleanest or most comfortable way to travel, but it was certainly the most romantic when it came to feeling that fully satisfied sense of having departed, journeyed and arrived, and of having been hauled by visible power.

The advent of the diesel has destroyed the visual charm of the train, whilst leaving what is left of rail travel relatively unimpaired, so that it remains – with the possible exception in the future, of the airship – the only spiritually uplifting way to make a journey. There is little joy or aesthetiscism in the motor car, whilst to be hurled through the skies at high speed and out of sight altitude in a claustrophobic, clinical pencil is less exciting and not nearly as dangerous as riding a bicycle round blind corners in a pedestrian precinct.

Life inconsiderately ended my train-spotting days, long before I entered my father's photographic business in Worcester. Had it been otherwise, *Vanishing Points* might have embraced an earlier, happier period of railway history.

Despite the first two family homes being within sight and sound of the railway, I was, for various reasons, unable to take advantage of such convenient locations. At the height of boyhood enthusiasm I had no camera and the nearest approach to a railway photograph was a paper negative of my brother's 'O' gauge Hornby. It was, in fact, my first photograph of any sort. Later on, as a professional, the volume and variety of photographic work left little time for trackside attendance, so that it was three working years before I photographed my first steam train, whilst the following eleven years produced but a handful of railway subjects.

Only after returning to Worcester from a four year period in London did I realise that the old, familiar railway sights, sounds and smells were about to be taken away. Suitably motivated, I spent as much time as possible in photographing last gasps of official steam operations in the area. It was no more than a belated piece of self-indulgence, designed solely to provide me with personal souvenirs.

By this time, in late 1963, my photographic outlook had undergone change. In earlier days the aim had been – wherever possible – to select the best time of the right kind of day, but having missed out on some prime crimes of architectural destruction in Worcester had taught me that events didn't wait for the weather to cheer up. My

First photograph – taken at the age of about twelve. A paper negative, using a home-made pinhole camera.

First railway photograph. A 2800 class, No. 3846 with an express freight at Norton Junction on 23rd September, 1952.

views on what to photograph had also changed, leading to the conclusion that the more mundane the subject the worthier it was of attention. It is, after all, the small incidents that often assume later significance, for all that they may initially be overlooked.

When steam finally departed, the collection totalled something in excess of two thousand photographs and I had absolutely no thought of it proving of interest to others. It was only when – at the suggestion of the former Worcester City Librarian and Curator, Cyril Phipps – I mounted the exhibition, 'Vanishing Points', that I began to appreciate how many devotees the railway had. The exhibition proved so popular that it made several further appearances at other venues. It should, of course, have been obvious to me that a public so cruelly and arbitrarily deprived of the living thing would hasten to mourn over lingering images of the loved one.

This was roughly nineteen years ago, when, elated by the response, I turned my attention to publishers, naïvely convinced that they would eagerly welcome the photographs. I was wrong, as evidenced by a typical editorial 'put-down': 'What our readers want is fact and not impression.' Sadly, I hid the photographs away – it seemed the decent thing to do in those chastening circumstances. Clearly, such rejections were the statutory penalty for being a photographer with urges to photograph the railway, as opposed to being a proper railway photographer.

When Alan Sutton asked me to go and see him, earlier this year, it had nothing to do with railway photographs, but I resurrected a few to include in a hastily gathered-together selection of prints to show him. Looking at them, he asked, 'Why haven't these been published before?' So, I told him. Surprisingly, he seemed not the least upset by my self-confessed ignorance of railway technicalities and promptly suggested the production of this book.

Provided his enthusiasm has not been misplaced, *Vanishing Points* will be a triumph for beginner's luck, for not only is it my first book and the book of my first exhibition, but it also includes my first photograph and first railway photograph. Above all, it is the direct result of my first crossing of a publisher's threshold.

Michael Dowty
Stoulton
1st December, 1985

VANISHING POINTS

'Your young men shall see visions' (Joel 2:28). Spotters at Railway Walk, Worcester. 25th October, 1953.

'Your old men shall dream dreams' (Joel 2:28). New Street, Birmingham. 27th October, 1953.

Spotters and the spotted. New Street, Birmingham. 27th October, 1953.

Early afternoon at New Street, Birmingham, on 27th October, 1953. The standing Jubilee class is No. 45597 *Barbados*.

The Midland line at Spetchley. Another favourite haunt of spotters. In this undated view, a Fowler 4F stands beneath the more northerly of two road bridges, awaiting the 'all clear'.

On the Norton embankment in February, 1954. Castle class, No. 4092, *Tresco Abbey* with a morning Worcester–Paddington express.

Collett 2251 class, No. 2241 at Bromyard Road, Worcester, with new sections for bridge replacement. 11th April, 1954.

Free Sunday morning entertainment for a silent, appreciative audience, as a crane lowers a girder into position on the Bromyard Road rail bridge. It could almost be a 'still' from an Ealing comedy. 11th April, 1954.

The Severn rail bridge at Worcester, 4th February, 1955. The original bridge was opened in May, 1860. It was replaced in 1906, but retains its original centre support. The Manor is unidentifiable and is seen backing towards Henwick station, about half a mile away.

Back in the '50s this old piece of G.W.R. road transport was to be seen rotting in a field near Pershore, looking not unlike something 'shot-up' by the Indians in some other Western setting. Labelled 'Express Parcels Services Paddington Station 6162', it eventually vanished from the scene. Today, not far away, there stands a more modern relic of railway–road links, painted a cheerful yellow and bearing the legend: 'Best Red Potatoes'. 8th December, 1957.

Early morning by the canal at Lowesmoor, Worcester, on 6th October, 1956. Some years later an attempt to repeat the view ended in failure after a wait of an hour or more saw only the passing of one steam locomotive – coasting downhill, with no head of steam and no sunshine.

This pretty and seemingly harmless scene was in reality the beginnings of an embankment fire at Malvern Link Common on 21st June, 1959.

Although the alarm had been quickly raised, the fire was rapidly spreading by the time the appliance arrived to get it under control.

Approaching Christmas on the Paddington–Worcester, this unknown little girl gave her doll a not too clear view of the passing landscape through a condensation-streaked window. 21st December, 1959.

Spotters, 'standers', passers-by and posters at an almost deserted Euston. 4th February, 1961.

At King's Cross, 11th February, 1961. A3 class, No. 60105 *Victor Wild*.

King's Cross Station on 11th February, 1961. From left – A4 class, No. 60006, *Sir Ralph Wedgwood*; Brush type 2, No. 5651; B1 class, No. 61406.

Two views of A4 class, No. 60017, *Silver Fox* at King's Cross. 7th June, 1961.

Minutes out from Shrub Hill, Worcester, Castle class No. 7027, *Thornbury Castle* at speed on the Norton embankment, heading for Paddington. 8th April, 1962.

County class No. 1002, *County of Berks* at Paddington in March, 1963.

A westbound freight at Henwick Road, Worcester, headed by a 5700 class, No. 8793, 23rd January, 1964. Maintenance work is being carried out on the signals. Henwick station was demolished four years later, leaving only the signal box. The crossing gates have long since been replaced by continental barriers.

Sky-fillers at Little Southfield Street, Worcester, with a westbound freight approaching Foregate Street station. 2nd February, 1964.

The 85A sheds, 5th February, 1964. A typical, simmering scene at Shrub Hill, Worcester, from the lower end of Railway Walk. By this time, more and more locomotives were suffering the indignity of running minus nameplates, numberplates – or both. The only identifiable specimen in this view is the foreground Castle, No. 7013, *Bristol Castle*.

An unidentified 2800 class, with a train of empties at Hampton Lovett, north of Droitwich on the Worcester–Birmingham line. 12th May, 1964.

Shrub Hill sheds on 15th June, 1964. The foreground line-up has a 5101 class, No. 4147, an unidentified pannier tank and Castle class, No. 7023, *Penrice Castle*. At the near corner of the left hand shed is Grange class, No. 6857, *Tudor Grange*.

Like the above view, this was taken from Railway Walk, though from a slightly higher altitude. To the left of the Worcester–Birmingham line are the carriage and wagon repair shops. Few of the locomotives are recognisable: nearest the camera is a B.R. 9F class, No. 92137, looking decidedly the worse for wear after a comparatively short time in service. To its right, on the nearer road, is Hall class, No. 6957, *Norcliffe Hall*.

Comprehensive view of the Shrub Hill layout from directly above the Tunnel Hill tunnel-mouth. A train of empties is seen heading for the out-of-sight yards on the left. The Birmingham–Hereford line curves away to the right, with the Malverns and Worcester Cathedral as a backdrop. The prominent, light-coloured building is not a church, but new plant at the gasworks. 15th June, 1964.

No. 7023, *Penrice Castle*, partly hidden by the cab and bunker of a 2-6-2T 6100 class, No. 6169. In the background is a pannier tank fitted with spark arrester chimney. The Hall standing behind it is almost certainly No. 6962, *Soughton Hall*. 15th June, 1964.

Jubilee class, No. 45674, *Duncan*, climbing away from Tunnel Hill at Astwood, Worcester, heading for Birmingham. 15th June, 1964.

No. 7011, *Banbury Castle* and fascinatingly fantastic foreground provided by the perennially unkempt bank of Railway Walk. 15th June, 1964.

Introduction to Bromyard station, three days before the official farewell. A small girl sharing a weed-encrusted platform with a pair of re-railing ramps. The posters behind extol the virtues of (left to right) Bournemouth, Colwyn Bay, Weston-Super-Mare and Littlehampton, all shortly to be unreachable by rail from the Bromyard Line. 3rd September, 1964.

A gloom of passengers and a dowdy Bedlington terrier awaiting the arrival of their train. On either side of the Booking Office entrance, identical posters – in the worst possible taste – urge: 'Give Dad a Break from that Steering-Wheel . . . take him out on a day trip – by train'. 3rd September, 1964.

The militant non-traveller. Although a train was signalled, this lady – flowers in one hand, aggressively-held, rolled umbrella in the other – had walked the visible length of track before ascending the platform-end and disappearing through the station exit.

The train from Worcester having arrived, there is a burst of activity – alighting and boarding, putting on jackets and searching for tickets.

The Unsmiling Cavalier: Leading Porter, Mr R. Pullen, posing alongside further imminently unreachable poster destinations.

Bromyard station staff: left to right, Station-master, Mr N.W.H. Bowkett; Leading Porter, Mr R. Pullen; Signalman, Mr G.M. Soley. 3rd September, 1964.

Bromyard's remaining railway.

The penultimate early morning train at Leigh Court station in fog and gloom. 4th September, 1964.

No. 8793 at Leigh Court, awaiting a barely visible 'All Clear'.

Disappearing into the fog on its way to Worcester.

Leigh Court station, already wearing an abandoned and neglected look on the day before its official closure. 4th September, 1964.

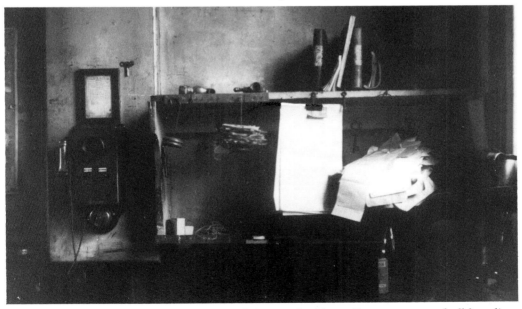

Knightwick station's office, complete with all the standard ingredients: papers on bulldog-clips, spiked receipts, keys on nails, telephone numbers pencilled on the wall, some half-empty bottles, a pewter pot and a jumbled piece of string. 4th September, 1964.

Bromyard station, rendered virtually invisible on closure day as No. 8793 prepares to depart with the final early morning work train. 5th September, 1964.

The station yard and its furniture.

Commendable British Rail thoroughness made sure that the cobwebs were in position in good time for the closure. 5th September, 1964.

No. 2232 being equipped with pre-departure decorations.

The last train ride from Bromyard, 6th September, 1964. Arranged by Bill Morris, a local coach proprietor, this took place the day after branch closure. If we, as a nation, take our pleasures sadly, we also know how to extract the maximum enjoyment from our sadnesses. At 7.30 a.m. Bromyard station was in all probability experiencing its busiest ever scene as passengers awaited the arrival of the ten-coach train. At the platform is Collett 2251 class, No. 2232 which was to pilot No. 2222 as far as Worcester.

8 a.m. departure in brilliant sunshine. Dramatic sky and dazzling fields in sharp contrast as the double-header gathers speed out of Bromyard.

Nos. 2232 and 2222 crossing the bridge to enter Knightwick station and pick up more passengers, having already stopped at Suckley. In the distance is a glimpse of the Teme Valley.

Decorations holding up
well as the train
approaches the bridge
at Bransford.

Blinding early morning sunshine at Henwick Road level crossing. Nos. 2232 and 2222 were
relieved at Shrub Hill where they were replaced by a Black Five No. 44691 which carried the 600
passengers on to Blackpool.

7th September, 1964. Smaller lettering on the poster offers: 'Unique opportunity of being Britain's first "Railway Beauty Queen" (chosen en route).' This is Margaret Millward with her crown, the day after it was placed on her head. She smiles, despite the undoubted bewilderment of being (possibly) the only queen to 'rule' a dead subject. Margaret was also facing the imminent irony of starting a course at Worcester's new Technical College and of having to travel there – by bus!

Leominster, 21st September, 1964. Collett 1400 class, No. 1420 shunting at the age of thirty one. A year later it was to be found at Worcester (one of the last locomotives to be overhauled there), restored to its original G.W.R. livery, prior to taking up residence on the Dart Valley Railway.

The crossing-keeper's signal box at
Wadborough station (Midland Region).

The lady crossing-keeper in action – a demanding, repetitive job, with an involved safety
procedure to be carried out, usually for a single vehicle at a time on a not very busy road.
22nd September, 1964.

Churchward churchward.

5101 class, No. 4107 leaving Gloucester for Ross-on-Wye, 22nd September, 1964. Passenger services on this line ended a little over a month later.

Gloucester, 22nd September, 1964. The 5.30 p.m. stopping train to Bristol taking on mail at platform 3.

Early evening silhouettes on a passenger footbridge at Gloucester. 22nd September, 1964.

24th September, 1964. Grange class No. 6837, *Forthampton Grange* with a morning express freight at Droitwich.

The Droitwich Station Scandal. In the middle of the month, British Rail decided to demolish all the buildings on the Birmingham platform, without (true to form) consulting anyone, merely stating that the buildings had dry-rot and that no replacement shelter would be provided. Peter Walker, M.P., sent a telegram to Dr Beeching, but he was 'on leave' and unavailable for comment. Apparently, the station-master was also 'on leave' and knew nothing of the semi-destruction of his station until his return. In the photograph, passengers are seen enjoying the wide, open spaces on an especially crisp 24th September morning.

No. 6986, *Rydal Hall* at Norton.

No. 5936, *Oakley Hall* passing Eckington station with a through freight as passengers board a local train from Cheltenham. 3rd October, 1964.

Alvechurch station with several unidentified 0-4-0 'Perambulator' class conveyances. 10th October, 1964.

Bromsgrove station on the morning of 10th October, 1964. A southbound stopping train, headed by Black Five No. 45006, departing past a north-bound freight awaiting banking assistance up Lickey.

The same freight passing through Bromsgrove station to begin the Lickey ascent.

Ring-a-ring-a-roses. 17th October, 1964.

How do they begin to sort this little lot out? Platform 1 at King's Cross, perfectly demonstrating one of the side effects of Beeching's Axe. As branch-line stations closed, more and more parcels and mail had to be handled at mainline stations. In this frantic scene there are seven men, invisibly struggling with the problem. 17th October, 1964.

Spotters at New Southgate, London, illustrating the bicycle's value as an aid to recognition. Not, perhaps, that there is much left worth recognising. 18th October, 1964.

The King's Cross problem on a smaller, more peaceful scale at Ross-on-Wye, two days before the withdrawal of passenger services. 29th October, 1964.

Canopy architecture from the footbridge steps at Ross-on-Wye.

The view from a different bridge: the church and farm buildings at Ashchurch, near Tewkesbury. 29th October, 1964.

Anyone for tennis? 30th October, 1964.

Token work at Longhope. 30th October, 1964.

Longhope signal box, with potted sideline.

2-6-2T. No. 4107 leaving Mitcheldean with an afternoon train for Ross-on-Wye. 30th October, 1964.

Too English for words – too English to last. The inoffensive country goods train, glimpsed near Longhope. 30th October, 1964.

Shrub Hill Road, Worcester. 2nd November, 1964. One of the two road traffic control signals for the old Hill Evans Vinegar Works Line which had two ungated crossings, the other one being in Pheasant Street where the factory was situated. The Railway Arms no longer exists, its site and those of other old properties now being occupied by the car park of a D.I.Y. establishment. (See also bottom of page 117.)

The now impossible view of Shrub Hill station's façade. At the time this was taken, the preliminaries were underway for the construction of the misnamed and ill-placed 'Elgar House'. It was as if some failed architectural surgeon had said 'Screens, please, Nurse; this patient mustn't be seen.' 2nd November, 1964.

Talking of Elgar; two days later, on 4th November, No. 7005, *Sir Edward Elgar* was nose to nose with No. 5000, *Launceston Castle* on Worcester's locomotive 'Death Row'. (See also pp. 62 and 139.)

New Street station, Birmingham, open to the sky during its re-development, with a 1950 Stanier 5MT No. 44691 filling much of the available space with an excess of steam. 7th November, 1964.

New Street, Birmingham. At the other end of the station a suspicious-looking traveller sits, caged in trolleys. It is, of course, extremely bad form for photographers to be 'spotted' by their victims. 7th November, 1964.

8th November, 1964. No. 6961 *Stedham Hall* at Worcester Shed, sporting its 81A (Old Oak Common) shed plate. At the top left of the photograph is part of the local spotters' paradise, Railway Walk.

Collett 5700 class, No. 4613 at its home shed, Worcester, on 8th November, 1964. No doubt shortly destined to make its final journey.

4-6-2 Britannia class, No. 70044, *Earl Haig*, appropriately putting in an appearance at Worcester at remembrance time. 8th November, 1964.

Two views of Stoulton station, between Worcester and Pershore, as it appeared on 11th November, 1964. In the first, it is deserted; in the second, obscured. Now, it isn't there at all. It was a few hundred yards north of here that the December 1984 derailment occurred (see bottom of page 129), the track by then having been singled.

NO TITLE. Years ago, it was a popular photographic cliché to display or publish photographs under this title – possibly as an escape clause for those with mental blocks. Here, its use is legitimate, with No. 7005, having days ago been stripped of its title, standing moodily in the shed as one of its nameplates is carried away to a safe place. On the left is Nick de Capa, who was described as being a 'tube mopper' (extensive subsequent enquiries have failed to establish the meaning of the term), whilst Loco Fitter, R. Waters is on the right. 17th November, 1964. It may be of interest that Sir Edward himself died within a very short distance of the Worcester Sheds, on 23rd February, 1934, at his home, 'Marl Bank', Rainbow Hill.

The Eckington footstool – a gracious and uplifting experience. 12th December, 1964. The Eckington platform being on the low side for comfort and convenience, the powers that were had thoughtfully provided stools for those in need of less strenuous ascent. Unhappily, old world charm furnishes an inadequate excuse for survival – station and footstool were chopped, less than a month later, together with the neighbouring stations of Bredon, Defford and Wadborough.

Surplus to requirements. . . . Tim Quiney, Porter at Defford station for more than thirty years, facing a bleak future as he poses on the last day of passenger services. Mr Quiney died not many years later and this photograph is intended as a memorial to him and many others whose years of loyalty were rewarded by nothing in particular. 2nd January, 1965.

At Bredon station, 2nd January, 1965. No. 7808, *Cookham Manor* with an express freight, heading towards Cheltenham and about to pass an anonymous unclassifiable 4-6-0.

Cookham Manor again, travelling at a fair pace and – in common with most named locomotives by now – minus its nameplates. Bredon, 2nd January, 1965.

Bredon again, with the now famous *Clun Castle* hurrying past with what appears to be a coal train. A bit of a come-down for No. 7029, which has since become one of the most photographed locomotives of the 'pickled steam' era. 2nd January, 1965.

Foregate Street, Worcester, on 6th January, 1965, featuring (left) the not long introduced 0-2-0 'traffic warden' class. The attractive bridge now carries a fraction of its former volume of rail traffic, thanks to progress, whilst the city becomes ever more choked with cars and restrictions. In this view, the dreaded yellow lines haven't yet appeared. It would be interesting to know how much paint is used, annually, in order to deface British roads.

Identical twins, out in the cold, cold snow. A pair of 2-6-2T 5101 class heading a freight through a wintry Norton Halt. The pilot is unidentifiable; the other is No. 4161. 3rd March, 1965.

Norton Halt in decline, reduced from its former 'Junction' status and soon to become nothing at all. The writing (and the drawing) is on the wall.

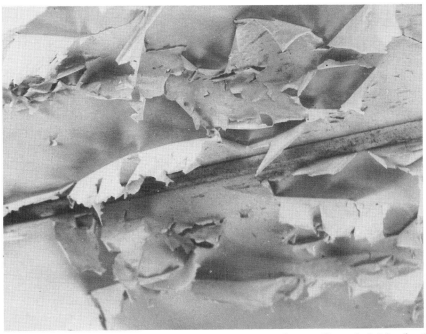

Norton Halt in decline (Part 2). The unappealing peeling ceiling. 3rd March, 1965.

Dirty-looking Collett with a smoke-stained smoke-stack (apologies to John Masefield). 2251 class, No. 2244 on an equally dirty day at Norton. 22nd March, 1965.

LAST SPRING. Two Black Fives, one black lamb and a few white-faced sheep. No. 44856 piloting No. 45311 at Norton. 23rd March, 1965.

Plenty of room overhead. Collett 2251 class at Norton, minus numberplate and barely recognisable by faint figures chalked on the cab side: 2222. 24th March, 1965.

The railbridge over Rainbow Hill, Worcester, looking down towards the city centre, 26th March, 1965. The poster on the left is for the Winston Churchill Memorial Appeal, Sir Winston having died in January.

27th March, 1965. The renowned *Clun Castle* at Worcester. Having taken on coal and water, it is about to rejoin its Ian Allen Rail Tour 'Special' at Shrub Hill station, with every move recorded – in one way or another – by the inevitable army of supporters.

The geometry of a dangerous game. Any number of boys running on parallel lines may never meet again. 24th April, 1965 – not that the date is of vital importance, except to the writer of a possible obituary.

On the 29th May, 1965, the Flying Scotsman was seen in Worcestershire, hauling the R.C.T.S. 'East Midlander'. When it passed Spetchley it was about half an hour late and dusk had arrived, making it almost too dark to photograph.

6100 class, No. 6147 approaching Shrub Hill station with a local passenger train. In the foreground are condemned locomotives, of which only No. 6958 *Oxburgh Hall* (centre) is identifiable. 25th June, 1965.

The same train, entering the station. The scaffolding in the background marks the growth of 'Elgar House' that now masks the station frontage.

More of the condemned: front left is No. 6829 *Burmington Grange*; to the right is No. 8415, one of Hawksworth's 9400 class of heavy shunters, introduced only in 1947. No. 8415 was one of the later versions, dating from 1949.

'For God's sake let us sit upon the ground and tell sad stories of the death of kings' (Richard II) . . . Castles, Halls, Granges, Manors, etc. Worcester, 1st July, 1965.

Worcester's two river bridges, seen from the cathedral tower, 3rd July, 1965. A westbound, diesel-hauled freight is barely visible in the distance, but the road bridge traffic is all too plain. The stretch of Severn in between has since been considerably tidied up, which is as well, because the two steamers appear to be moored almost in mid-stream.

A 5700 class, No. 3682 crossing the arches by Worcester cattle market. 5th July, 1965. (See also bottom of page 76.)

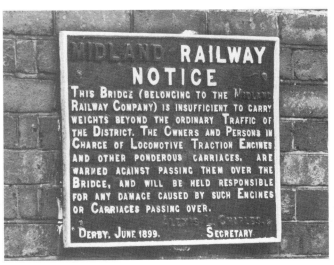

This notice at Defford raises a few questions: How many were in committee on the day it was decided that 'Midland' was a dirty word? What was the crime of Alexis L. Charles that led to the 'blacking' of his name? Finally, how large was the army of pot and brush men assigned to this formidable task of selective obliteration?

Malvern Wells station on 29th July, 1965. A 6100 class, No. 6169 with a train of empties. This was the last in the class, introduced in 1931 for London suburban working.

No. 3682 shunting near Malvern Link station on 30th July, 1965.

The religious background at Worcester. A local train pulling clear of Foregate Street station and climbing to Shrub Hill. St Andrew's spire (better known as 'The Glover's Needle' on account of the city's considerable former gloving industry) dominates the scene. To the right is St Nicholas Church.

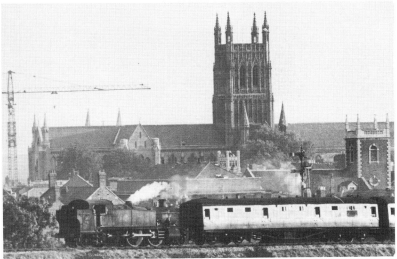

Dwarfed by Worcester Cathedral, the same train catches some early evening sunlight. On the extreme right is Old St Martin's Church. The crane on the left is at work on the construction of the new Lichgate shopping precinct and Giffard Hotel. 17th August, 1965.

19th August, 1965. An express freight approaching and passing the signal box at Norton. Despite Norton's reduced status having lowered it from 'Junction' to 'Halt', the signal-box still carries its 'Junction' title, perhaps for fairly obvious reasons.

The same freight passing Norton Halt. Heading it is a 2800 class, No. 3863.

Norton Halt again. The grimy Hall could just possibly be No. 6950 *Kingthorpe Hall*.
19th August, 1965.

Stourport-on-Severn power station: a small shunter being made to appear even smaller by a pylon trio. 7th September, 1965.

Worcester, Shrub Hill. Tranquility behind the sheds, with enterprising railmen's onions sunning themselves on a corrugated roof. 13th September, 1965.

Rainbow Hill Junction Signal Box. Grange class No. 6827, *Llanfrechfa Grange*, running light, backing past the box whilst 'looping', a familiar operation at Worcester in the absence of a turntable. 13th September, 1965.

Having turned itself round, *Llanfrechfa Grange* heads north on the Birmingham line, emerging from behind one of the sheds and about to pass the back of the coaling-stage.

Smokey zone. 13th September, 1965.

Warm front. 13th September, 1965.

Smokeless zone. 13th September, 1965.

Hot shoe. 15th September, 1965.

83

Higher steam. 13th September, 1965.

Cooling shower. 15th September, 1965.

Gentle exercise. 15th September, 1965.

Lower steam. 15th September, 1965.

Simmering at the sheds. No. 7907 *Hart Hall* behind No. 3682, with the inevitable *Clun Castle* poking its nose in on the extreme right. 13th September, 1965.

Further simmerings. On the left is No. 6900 *Witherslack Hall*, and behind the anonymous pannier tank is a 5MT No. 45388. 16th September, 1965.

The crossing and signal-box at Littleton and Badsey.

It was at Littleton and Badsey that Mr J. Allchurch (no doubt prompted by the fact that a diesel had broken down on the previous day) related the following poignant incident: 'We were on holiday in Cornwall, the wife and me, and we climbed a hill to a little museum, and inside there was this steam nameplate. I stood, looking at it, and the wife said to me, "Why, you're crying, you've got tears in your eyes". "Well", I said, "there's more metal in that plate than there is in the whole of one of these diesels."' 15th September, 1965.

Looking forward to no future? 16th September, 1965.

A 5700 class, No. 3615 at the entrance to the Carriage and Wagon Works, managing to obscure the identity of the Diesel Railcar with a steamy burst of enthusiasm. 16th September, 1965.

Leaping down lightly into oblivion. 16th
September, 1965.

One worker, several retired.
17th September, 1965.

Restored to former glory. 1906 Churchward 4500 class, No. 4555, with 1932 Collett 1400 class, No. 1420 standing at Worcester Shed. Both were shortly to take up residence on the Dart Valley Railway. 19th September, 1965. (See also page 44 and top of page 136.)

Also on 19th September, a strange visitor was to be seen at Worcester Shed: preserved L.N.E.R. No. 3442 *The Great Marquess,* seen here framed by the shed entrance and then from the north entrance to the tunnel.

Emerging from Tunnel Hill, 4555, piloting 1420 with a six coach 'special'. 19th September, 1965.

20th September, 1965. Seen from the footbridge at Railway Walk, an unknown Hall putting plenty of effort into the climb to Shrub Hill as it emerges from Foregate Street station.

A westbound passenger train leaving Shrub Hill station, describing an exaggerated curve as it heads for Foregate Street. 20th September, 1965.

Again from the Railway Walk footbridge, a B.R. Standard class, No. 75000 sporting rather splendid steam whiskers. 20th September, 1965.

Return to the onion industry. More fine specimens drying on the roof and providing something for a forlorn-looking Grange to cry over. 20th September, 1965.

Four late impressions of working steam at Shrub Hill. 20th & 21st September, 1965.

31st December, 1965. On a dark and drizzling day, steam operations officially ended at Worcester. There were few people and little steam present to mark the occasion . . . just a little indoor paper-work . . .

. . . and some outdoor paper-buying . . .

. . . a single figure crossing the tracks . . .

. . . and a heartfelt message symbolising the double-crossing of those who read between the lines.

DOOMDAY. Netherton Churchyard, Dudley.

Going off duty; the uphill trudge in Railway Walk. 6th February, 1966.

Though officially no more, steam was still to be seen fairly often at Worcester for a few more months. This morning view looks over the roof of a locomotive shed directly onto Shrub Hill Station. Under clear conditions it was possible to see almost as far as Norton from this viewpoint. 3rd February, 1966.

By now, working steam had all but vanished from the Worcester scene. This view was from the road bridge in Comer Road, St John's. 29th April, 1966.

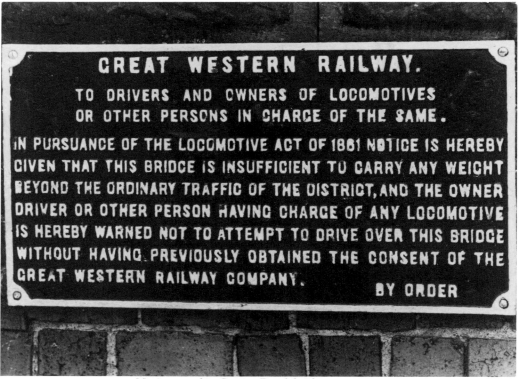

GREAT WESTERN RAILWAY.

TO DRIVERS AND OWNERS OF LOCOMOTIVES OR OTHER PERSONS IN CHARGE OF THE SAME.

IN PURSUANCE OF THE LOCOMOTIVE ACT OF 1861 NOTICE IS HEREBY GIVEN THAT THIS BRIDGE IS INSUFFICIENT TO CARRY ANY WEIGHT BEYOND THE ORDINARY TRAFFIC OF THE DISTRICT, AND THE OWNER DRIVER OR OTHER PERSON HAVING CHARGE OF ANY LOCOMOTIVE IS HEREBY WARNED NOT TO ATTEMPT TO DRIVE OVER THIS BRIDGE WITHOUT HAVING PREVIOUSLY OBTAINED THE CONSENT OF THE GREAT WESTERN RAILWAY COMPANY.

BY ORDER

Notice on the Comer Road bridge parapet.

A good, old-fashioned road sign at Hartlebury.

30th April, 1966. Hartlebury station: a picture-book piece of railway architecture – until the desecration of July, 1971. (See pages 122 and 123.)

Great Western and proud of it – even if
nothing else remains of the station.
Stoulton, 14th May, 1966.

The early stages of demolition at Shrub Hill. 15th June, 1966.

Midland and ashamed – and such a pretty setting, too! The word has been painted-out in three places, as has also the name of James Williams, clearly deemed to be as unworthy of recognition as Alexis L. Smith. Wadborough, 17th May, 1966.

Ashchurch station with its impressive platform canopies. 7th July, 1966.

Ashchurch station. The bright and spacious waiting room, with its patterned floor, vase of moderately fresh flowers and commendably varied selection of tidily arranged magazines. 7th July, 1966.

Cast-iron economy at Pershore station. Heavily fractured notice given added support. 7th July, 1966.

A magnificent and exciting, self-praising poster by Pershore station entrance. Just the thing to cheer the arriving passenger as he ponders the law of diminishing returns – and singles. 7th July, 1966.

Shrub Hill. The cab of a Midland 3F. 0-6-0T. No. 47681, awaiting its inevitable fate. 14th July, 1966.

Strange companions at Shrub Hill, providing temporary light relief from the general air of desolation. 14th July, 1966.

The literal 'Vanishing Points', at an overgrown Stourbridge, during a visit officially concerned with photographing the demolition of the nearby gasworks. 26th July, 1966.

Worcestershire supporters stand at Shrub Hill station in seven minutes to seven o'clock shadow, waiting for the train taking them to Lord's for the Gillette Cup Final against Warwickshire. Their early morning enthusiasm was misplaced – Worcestershire lost. 3rd September, 1966.

A spot of mystery and excitement – a body on the line and distant drums. Shrub Hill, 2nd October, 1966.

Demolition time at Littleton and Badsey. A collection of familiar railway bits and pieces. 11th October, 1966.

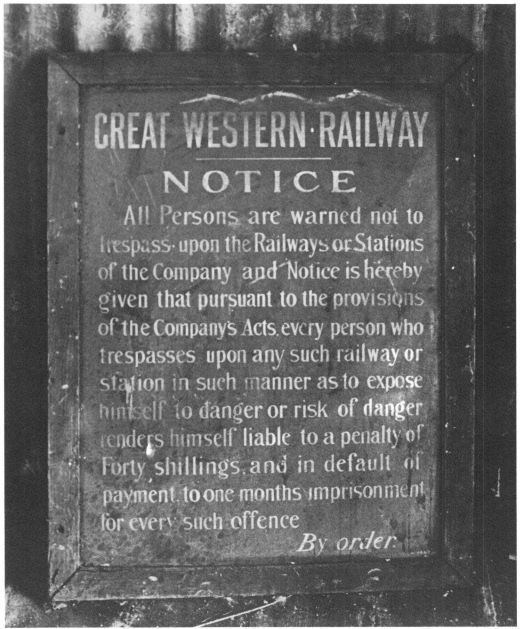

A wooden notice at Littleton and Badsey, of such seeming antiquity that its authenticity is almost questionable. 11th October, 1966.

B.R.'s Sheeting Works at Shrub Hill, gutted by fire. 16th October, 1967.

Passengers awaiting rescue by road transport at the entrance to Shrub Hill station. 'Elgar House' is by now screening the view of the city, though it may have its uses as a draught-excluder on cold days. 14th July, 1967.

The family connection (not with the fire on the preceding page). Elizabeth, Fiona and Bridget arriving at Shrub Hill to catch the London train on 19th August, 1968. Elizabeth is making sure she has the tickets; Fiona is (apparently) singing; Bridget is silently observant.

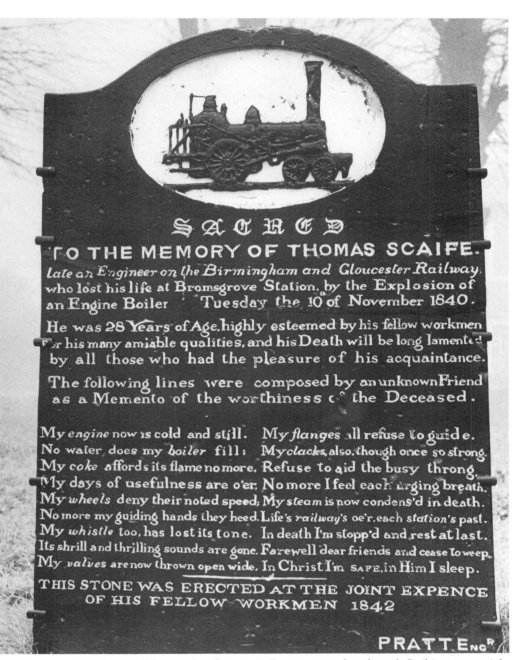

SACRED
TO THE MEMORY OF THOMAS SCAIFE.
late an Engineer on the Birmingham and Gloucester Railway,
who lost his life at Bromsgrove Station, by the Explosion of
an Engine Boiler   Tuesday the 10 of November 1840.

He was 28 Years of Age, highly esteemed by his fellow workmen
For his many amiable qualities, and his Death will be long lamented
by all those who had the pleasure of his acquaintance.

The following lines were composed by an unknown Friend
as a Memento of the worthiness of the Deceased.

My engine now is cold and still.   My flanges all refuse to guide.
No water does my boiler fill;   My clacks, also, though once so strong,
My coke affords its flame no more.   Refuse to aid the busy throng,
My days of usefulness are o'er.   No more I feel each urging breath.
My wheels deny their noted speed;   My steam is now condens'd in death.
No more my guiding hands they heed.   Life's railway's oe'r. each station's past.
My whistle too, has lost its tone.   In death I'm stopp'd and rest at last.
Its shrill and thrilling sounds are gone.   Farewell dear friends and cease to weep.
My valves are now thrown open wide.   In Christ I'm SAFE, in Him I sleep.

THIS STONE WAS ERECTED AT THE JOINT EXPENCE
OF HIS FELLOW WORKMEN   1842

PRATT. Eng.ᴿ

11th January, 1969. The well-known headstones in Bromsgrove churchyard. Striking memorials to Thomas Scaife and Joseph Rutherford, both of whom were killed by the explosion of their engine boiler at Bromsgrove station on 10th November, 1840. Rutherford actually died on the following day.

115

Open Day at Shrub Hill on 12th April, 1969. Sir Gerald Nabarro with 'Miss Rail News'.

British Rail proudly showing off its new image, with some small concession to steam (7808 *Cookham Manor*). Altogether, a cheerful and lively enough event, but . . .

. . . just across the not so permanent way is the newly-created B.R. wasteland, not quite so much to crow about. 12th April, 1969.

SHRUB HILL ROAD LEVEL CROSSING.
NOTICE

Foot Passengers & Drivers of Vehicles along this Road are warned to observe the Signals on the Right hand side of the Road.

When the arm is in this position or when a RED light is shown, a train is about to cross & all traffic along the Road is **STOPPED.**

When the arm is in this position or a WHITE light is shown the Road is clear.

Photographed on 27th August, 1969 at the Transport Museum, Clapham, this notice will probably now be housed at York. It does seem to be frightfully wordy and complicated. Today's motorist with his growing inability to respond to a simple red light might well have trouble in taking in so much information all at once.

Signals and lamp at Henwick station, Worcester. 9th June, 1970.

Lansdowne Road, Cheltenham. Comings and goings on 9th May, 1970.

Solitary figure with solitary luggage.

2nd June, 1970. Pirton Crossing signal-box. Signalman Peter Figgett with visitor.

Peter Figgett, relaxed in his natural environment.

Signalman's view – from the box at Pirton Crossing.

Signalman's chart.

121

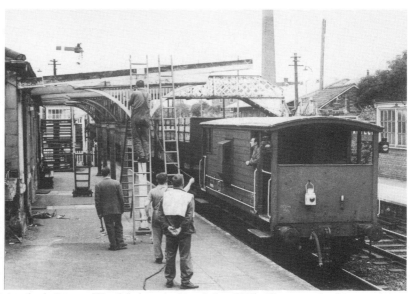

A small miscalculation at Hartlebury on 21st July, 1971. The guard of a passing train looks slightly apprehensive. The object of the exercise is to remove the platform canopy supports . . .

. . . but not in this direction. We are about to have another body on the line as the support decides to go its own way.

British Rail regrets the delay . . .

. . . Normal working will resume as soon as the inquest is over.

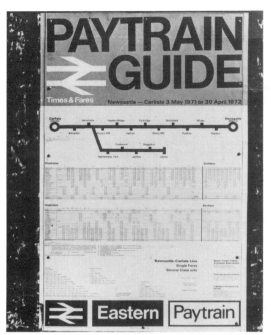

An assignment up north led to an introduction to the Paytrain, operating between Newcastle and Carlisle. This is the type of system which many felt could and should have been widely introduced as an alternative to senseless closures. 24th November, 1971.

An impressive quartet of cooling towers near Newcastle, viewed from a Paytrain.

Midday at Newcastle Central on 24th November, 1971.

Durham Cathedral, 24th November, 1971. The advance calculations for this view were made on the journey north, two days previously. They did not, however, take into account the intervening snowfall or the fact that the sun would be in the wrong part of the sky, or that the window would be filthy and that to risk opening it on such a bitterly cold day would certainly lead to an unscheduled lynching by fellow passengers.

Through glass darkly – a brief impression of Sheffield station. 24th November, 1971.

Replacing *Hagley Hall*'s nameplates at Bewdley on the Severn Valley Railway, 6th January, 1973. This finds its way onto the page by way of saying 'thank you' to Adrian Vaughan, author of a favourite railway book. In *Signalman's Twilight*, he recalls how No. 4930 took over from a failed diesel on 29th June, 1963, covering the 53½ miles from near Swindon to Paddington in 45 minutes, being timed at 82 m.p.h. at Didcot.

Driving home from an assignment in North Wales, this depressing sight of Llangollen station presented itself. Definitely nothing to sing about. 20th June, 1974.

Restored to its original L.M.S. livery and number, Jubilee class, No. 5690 *Leander* heading west over the canal at Lowesmoor, Worcester, with *The Midlander*. 5th October, 1974.

At the other end of the day, *Leander* on its return journey, approaching Bransford Road station at dusk, leaving the hazy Malverns behind. 5th October, 1974.

1st December, 1984. Clearing up after the previous day's derailment at Stoulton. Track singling may be fine in theory, when everything is running smoothly, but when this kind of thing happens it must prove a major headache. Cynics have long regarded singling operations as a prelude to eventual line closure.

Bristol Temple Meads, re-visited after something in excess of forty years as a personal, part-celebration of GW150. Still as impressive, despite having run out of steam, though with one small stain on its character for compelling its worshippers to join long queues at the Booking Hall, merely to purchase platform tickets in the absence of a sick machine.

Memorial tablet to Miss Emma Saunders, 'The Railwaymen's Friend', situated at the entrance to Temple Meads station. 29th March, 1985.

Tracks out of Temple Meads.

Easter Monday at Arley station on the Severn Valley Railway. 8th April, 1985. Proving, as always, that steam's public is undiminished. A Bewdley–Bridgnorth train is seen ariving on the left, as one of the railway's two Ivatt's, No. 46521 waits to move off with its Bridgnorth–Bewdley.

The other Severn Valley Ivatt, No. 46443 attracting plenty of attention at Arley. 8th April, 1985.

132

Happy Anniversary, G.W.R.! 28th July, 1985. On the weekend of official celebrations, this was the scene at Shrub Hill on an identical day to the dark and drizzling one that marked the end of steam at Worcester. The photograph shows the area at the back of the sheds which used to be better and more fully employed than this. Handy to have the extra car parking space, though.

The front of the Shrub Hill Sheds, revealing still more car parking facilities.
28th July, 1985.

3rd August, 1985. The Torbay & Dartmouth Railway at Kingswear. Preserved Manor class, No. 7827 *Lydham Manor* backing past some seaweed-covered boating relics to take up position to haul the 3.15 p.m. to Paignton.

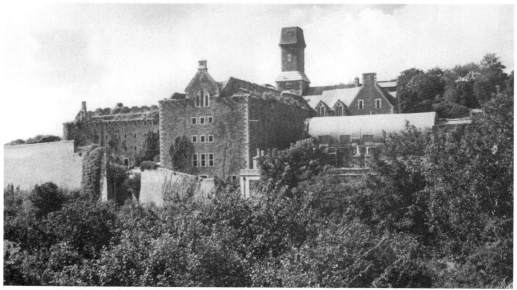

Bodmin Gaol, Cornwall, 6th August, 1985. One of the earliest standard gauge railways, the Bodmin–Wadebridge Railway, used to pass directly in front of the gaol, enabling spectators to arrive by train to witness public executions. The gaol closed in 1922, but part of it is open to the public and is well worth a visit.

Some of the most moving G.W.R. tributes were the floral ones featuring in cities and towns with Western associations. How the talents behind such displays managed to design, produce and maintain their creations throughout a memorably bad summer is a mystery. This one was at Plymouth. 7th August, 1985.

The Dart Valley Railway has a small museum at Buckfastleigh. This is the view from the footplate of one of the exhibits, a Southern tank, No. 3298. 10th August, 1985.

Buckfastleigh station on the D.V.R., 10th August, 1985. Churchward's 4500 class, No. 4555 about to leave with the last train of the day, the 3.45 to Totnes. (See also page 90 and bottom of page 91.)

Enthusiasm for the GW150 Exhibition Train's visit to Worcester, 4th September, 1985. This could well be the last time that Foregate Street station attracts a crowd of such proportions.

Many bookshops took the trouble to stage G.W.R. window displays, demonstrating the range of literature available to Western addicts. 'Something for a rainy day' would have been a fitting sub-theme in this soggy celebration year. The window shown here is that of 'Town Books and Toys', in Eastgate Street, Gloucester.

28th August, 1985. Brunel's Box. Not exactly what he would have envisaged as a future possibility, with the emergence of this strange, soulless creature from the mouth of his masterpiece. Otherwise, the scene is as English as ever it was.

Early evening in a Refreshment Room at Oxford. 11th September, 1985.

The 'Paddington' link at Bath. Cleverly planned and beautifully executed, this elaborate piece of floral artwork embodies the essential quality of the railway it commemorates – something to appeal to all ages. 12th September, 1985.

Full circle back to childhood things. On reflection, it may well have been this 'Cheltenham Flyer' jigsaw puzzle, produced by the G.W.R. in 1934, that first aroused railway interest. Apart from a set of building bricks and a couple of non-railway books, it is the sole survivor from early childhood. The box may have suffered a little, but the puzzle has entertained three generations. As for the 'Flyer', it has followed the 'Western' into the realms of memory. The motive power in the puzzle is No. 5000, *Launceston Castle*, better remembered in this way than in my photograph (page 86) of 4th November, 1964.

Vanishing point.